Books should be returned or renewed by the
last date stamped above

CHARTER MARK
Awarded for excellence
to Arts & Libraries

Kent County Council
EDUCATION & LIBRARIES

The Oscar Wilde Quotation Book

The Oscar Wilde Quotation Book

A Literary Companion

Edited by
GYLES BRANDRETH

ROBERT HALE • LONDON

Preface and selection © Gyles Brandreth 1995
First published in Great Britain 1995

ISBN 0 7090 5709 1

Robert Hale Limited
Clerkenwell House
Clerkenwell Green
London EC1R 0HT

The right of Gyles Brandreth to be identified
as author of this work has been asserted by him
in accordance with the Copyright, Designs
and Patents Act 1988.

2 4 6 8 10 9 7 5 3 1

Printed and bound in Great Britain
by WBC Book Manufacturers Ltd,
Bridgend, Mid Glamorgan.

Preface

Oscar Fingal O'Flahertie Wills Wilde was born in Dublin on 16 October 1854.

> My name has two 'O's', two 'F's' and two 'W's'. A name which is destined to be in everybody's mouth must not be too long. It comes so expensive in the advertisements. When one is unknown, a number of Christian names are useful, perhaps needful. As one becomes famous, one sheds some of them, just as a balloonist, when rising higher, sheds unnecessary ballast.

Wilde's father was a distinguished eye surgeon and seasoned philanderer, his mother, the daughter of an archdeacon, a poet and polemicist celebrated for her salon. Oscar was educated at Trinity College, Dublin, and Magdalen College, Oxford, where he was noted for his brilliance and his studied eccentricity. (In a viva voce exam he was required to translate the New Testament from the Greek. He did so with effortless fluency, and when he had completed the set passage the examiners asked him to stop. Wilde ignored them and

5

continued his translation. The examiners told him they were quite satisfied with his translation and there was no need to continue. 'Oh, do let me go on,' protested Oscar, 'I want to see how it ends.')

Having secured several prizes and a double First at Oxford, he floated to London and established a reputation as an aesthete, dilettante, occasional critic and poet. In 1881 his first volume of poems was published and he was satirized in Gilbert and Sullivan's opera Patience. In 1882 he set off for America, where he told the New York customs officers that he had nothing to declare but his genius. He later maintained that his lecture tour in the United States had been so successful that he had been obliged to employ two secretaries, one being responsible for requests for autographs, the other for requests for locks of his hair, and that in six months the first had died of writer's cramp and the other was completely bald.

In May 1884 Wilde married Constance Lloyd, the daughter of a Dublin lawyer, and they settled in Tite Street, Chelsea. They had two sons, Cyril, born in 1885, and Vyvyan, born in 1886. The Canterville Ghost and Lord Arthur Savile's Crime appeared in 1887 and, in 1888, he published The Happy Prince and other Tales, a collection of fabulous children's stories. His reputation rests largely on the four comedies he wrote between 1892 and 1895. His notoriety springs from his arrest and imprisonment in 1895, following the collapse of his ill-judged libel action against the Marquis of Queensberry who had accused Wilde of 'posing as a Somdomite' (sic). His contemporary, Frank Harris, observed, 'Oscar Wilde's greatest play was his own life. It was a five act tragedy with Greek implications and he was its most ardent spectator.'

Wilde came out of prison in May 1897 and published his last work, The Ballad of Reading Gaol, in February 1898. A ruined man, he lived his remaining years in France and died at the Hotel d'Alsace, 13 rue des beaux arts, on 30 November 1900.

On his tomb in the Père-Lachaise cemetery in Paris are four lines from The Ballad of Reading Gaol:

> And alien tears will fill for him
> Pity's long-broken urn,
> For his mourners will be outcast men,
> And outcasts always mourn.

Wilde's extraordinary and tragic story has been told in many biographies, from Robert Sherard's in 1906 to Richard Ellman's over eighty years later. There have also been several collections of Wilde's wit and wisdom, the best, I reckon, being Alvin Redman's Epigrams of Oscar Wilde, published in 1952 with the blessing of Wilde's younger son, Vyvyan Holland. My collection is different only in that the selection is my own and I have arranged the material as a kind of informal dictionary of wit. My hope is that, as you dip into it, you will get a proper flavour of the great man's way with words. By all accounts Wilde was a unique conversationalist. Bernard Shaw said, 'He was incomparably the greatest talker of his time – perhaps of all time.'

Yeats recalled his first meeting with Wilde as 'an astonishment'. 'I never before heard a man talking with perfect sentences, as if he had written them all overnight with labour and yet all spontaneous.' John Badley, an exact contemporary of Yeats and the founder of Bedales School, where Wilde's sons were pupils, told me (at around the time of his 100th birthday in 1965) that he believed much of Wilde's wit was 'studied'. Badley recalled saying at a house party in Cambridge with Oscar and travelling back with him to London by train. Assorted fellow guests came to the station to see Wilde and Badley on their way. At the moment the train was due to pull out, Wilde delivered a valedictory quip, then the guard blew the whistle and waved his green flag, the admirers on the platform cheered, Wilde sank back in his seat and the train moved off. Unfortunately, it only moved a yard or two before juddering to a halt. The group on the platform gathered again outside the compartment occupied by Badley and Wilde. Oscar hid behind his newspaper and hissed at his companion, 'They've had my parting shot. I only prepared one.'

Possibly Wilde did contrive some of his sparkling turns of phrase in advance, but of the extraordinary spontaneity of much of his wit there can be no doubt. On one occasion he boasted that he could talk on any subject that might be suggested to him. One of the party immediately proffered a possibility, 'the Queen'. Instantly Oscar responded, 'the Queen is not a subject.' He could be witty too in pretty trying circumstances. The story goes that a tax inspector called at the family house in Tite Street. 'Taxes!' exclaimed Wilde, 'Why should I pay taxes?'

'Are you not the householder here?' protested the tax inspector. 'You live here, you sleep here.'

'Ah, yes,' said Wilde, 'but then I sleep so badly!'

If proof were needed of Wilde's capacity for spontaneous wit, one only has to read the transcript of the three trials of 1895. When Wilde heard that he would be cross-examined by Edward Carson, who had been an undergraduate with him at Trinity College, Dublin, Oscar remarked, 'No doubt he will perform his task with all the added bitterness of an old friend.' There were moments during the cross-examination when Wilde was so brilliant and so witty that the dialogue seemed to spring from one of his own plays.

CARSON:	Did you become intimate with a young lad named Alphonse Conway at Worthing?
WILDE:	Yes.

CARSON:	He sold newspapers at the kiosk on the pier?
WILDE:	No, I never heard that up to that time his only occupation was selling newspapers. It is the first I have heard of his connection with literature . . . .

CARSON:	Did Charles Parker call you 'Oscar'?
WILDE:	Yes. I like to be called 'Oscar' or 'Mr Wilde'.
CARSON:	You had wine?
WILDE:	Of course.
CARSON:	Was there plenty of champagne?
WILDE:	Well, I did not press wine upon them.
CARSON:	You did not stint them?
WILDE:	What gentleman would stint his guests?

CARSON:	Do you drink champagne yourself?
WILDE:	Yes; iced champagne is a favourite drink of mine – strongly against my doctor's orders.
CARSON:	Never mind your doctor's orders, sir.
WILDE:	I never do.

At the second trial Wilde was cross-examined about two poems written by Lord Alfred Douglas and was questioned on the meaning of a particular phrase. Counsel asked, 'What is the "Love that dare not speak its name"?'

Without hesitation, Wilde replied,

'The Love that dare not speak its name' in this century is such a great affection of an elder for a younger man as there was between David and Jonathan, such as Plato made the very basis of his philosophy, and such as you find in the sonnets of

Michelangelo and Shakespeare. It is that deep, spiritual affection that is as pure as it is perfect. It dictates and pervades great works of art like those of Shakespeare and Michelangelo, and those two letters of mine, such as they are. It is in this century misunderstood, so much misunderstood that it may be described as the 'Love that dare not speak its name', and on account of it I am placed where I am now. It is beautiful, it is fine, it is the noblest form of affection. There is nothing unnatural about it. It is intellectual, and it repeatedly exists between an elder and a younger man, when the elder man has intellect, and the younger man has all the joy, hope and glamour of life before him. That it should be so the world does not understand. The world mocks at it and sometimes puts one in the pillory for it.

Max Beerbohm was in court. 'Oscar has been quite superb,' he reported.

His speech about the Love that dares not tell his name was simply wonderful and carried the whole court right away, quite a tremendous burst of applause. Here was this man, who had been for a month in prison and loaded with insults and crushed and buffeted, perfectly self-possessed, dominating the Old Bailey with his fine presence and musical voice.

I hope you will sense that presence and hear that voice in all the pages that follow.

GYLES BRANDRETH

Action
Action, indeed, is always easy, and when presented to us in its most aggravated, because most continuous, form, which I take to be that of real industry, becomes simply the refuge of people who have nothing whatever to do.
The Critic as Artist

Adoration
Being adored is a nuisance. Women treat us just as Humanity treats its Gods. They worship us and are always asking us to do something for them.
The Picture of Dorian Gray

Advice
I always pass on good advice. It is the only thing to do with it. It is never any use to oneself.
An Ideal Husband

People are very fond of giving away what they need most themselves. It is what I call the depths of generosity.
The Picture of Dorian Gray

Aesthetics
Ethics, like natural selection, make existence possible. Aesthetics, like sexual selection, make life lovely and wonderful, fill it with new forms, and give it progress, and variety and change.
The Critic as Artist

Age
As long as a woman can look ten years younger than her own daughter, she is perfectly satisfied.
The Picture of Dorian Gray

Don't be conceited about your bad qualities. You may lose them as you grow old.
A Woman of No Importance

Thirty-five is a very attractive age. London society is full of women of the very highest birth who have, of their own free choice, remained thirty-five for years.
The Importance of Being Earnest

The Ages of Man
The old believe everything; the middle-aged suspect everything; the young know everything.
Phrases and Philosophies for the Use of the Young

The pulse of joy that beats in us at twenty, becomes sluggish. Our limbs fail, our senses rot. We degenerate into hideous puppets, haunted by the memory of the passions of which we were too much afraid, and the exquisite temptations that we had not the courage to yield to. Youth! Youth! There is absolutely nothing in the world but youth!
The Picture of Dorian Gray

The soul is born old but grows young. That is the comedy of life. And the body is born young and grows old. That is life's tragedy.
A Woman of No Importance

Agreement
When people agree with me I always feel that I must be wrong.
The Critic as Artist

Ambition
Ambition is the last refuge of the failure.
Phrases and Philosophies for the Use of the Young

I have no ambition to be a popular hero, to be crowned
with laurels one year and pelted with stones the next; I
prefer dying peaceably in my own bed.
Vera, or The Nihilists

America and the Americans
We have really everything in common with America
nowadays, except, of course, language.
The Canterville Ghost

Many American ladies on leaving their native land adopt
an appearance of chronic ill-health, under the impression
that it is a form of European refinement.
The Canterville Ghost

Perhaps, after all, America never has been discovered. I
myself would say that it had merely been detected.
The Picture of Dorian Gray

The crude commercialism of America, its materialism
spirit, its indifference to the poetical side of things, and
its lack of imagination and of high unattainable ideas, are
entirely due to that country having adopted for its
national hero a man who, according to his own confession, was incapable of telling a lie, and it is not too much
to say that the story of George Washington and the cherry-tree has done more harm, and in a shorter space of
time, than any other moral tale in the whole of literature
– and the amusing part of the whole thing is that the
story of the cherry-tree is an absolute myth.
The Decay of Lying

'The say that when good Americans die they go to Paris,' chuckled Sir Thomas . . .

'Really! And where do bad Americans go to when they die?' inquired the Duchess.

'They go to America,' murmured Lord Henry.

The Picture of Dorian Gray

LADY CAROLINE: These American girls carry off all the good matches. Why can't they stay in their own country? They are always telling us it is the Paradise of Women.

LORD ILLINGWORTH: It is, Lady Caroline. That is why, like Eve, they are so extremely anxious to get out of it.

A Woman of No Importance

The youth of America is their oldest tradition. It has been going on now for three hundred years. To hear them talk we would imagine they were in their first childhood. As far as civilization goes they are in their second.

A Woman of No Importance

All Americans lecture . . . I suppose it is something in their climate.

A Woman of No Importance

LADY CAROLINE: There are a great many things you haven't got in America, I am told, Miss Worsley. They say you have no ruins, and no curiosities.

MRS ALLONBY: What nonsense! They have their mothers and their manners.

A Woman of No Importance

14

Appearance
It is only very ugly or very beautiful women who ever hide their faces.
The Duchess of Padua

Knaves nowadays do look so honest that honest folk are forced to look like knaves so as to be different.
The Duchess of Padua

A mask tells us more than a face.
Pen, Pencil and Poison

A really well-made buttonhole is the only link between Art and Nature.
Phrases and Philosophies for the Use of the Young

One should either be a work of art, or wear a work of art.
Phrases and Philosophies for the Use of the Young

The plain women are very useful. If you want to gain a reputation for respectability, you have merely to take them down to supper. The other women are very charming. They commit one mistake, however. They paint in order to try and look young. Our grandmothers painted in order to try and talk brilliantly.
The Picture of Dorian Gray

Her capacity for family affection is extraordinary. When her third husband died, her hair turned quite gold from grief.
The Picture of Dorian Gray

It is only the shallow people who do not judge by appearances.
The Picture of Dorian Gray

With an evening coat and a white tie, anybody, even a stockbroker, can gain a reputation for being civilized.
The Picture of Dorian Gray

There *is* a good deal to be said for blushing, if one can do it at the proper moment.
A Woman of No Importance

A woman whose size in gloves is seven and three-quarters never knows much about anything.
An Ideal Husband

She wore far too much rouge last night and not quite enough clothes. That is always a sign of despair in a woman.
An Ideal Husband

He has nothing, but looks everything. What more can one desire?
The Importance of Being Earnest

A well-tied tie is the first serious step in life.
The Importance of Being Earnest

Good looks are a snare that every sensible man would like to be caught in.
The Importance of Being Earnest

Argument
Arguments are extremely vulgar, for everybody in good society holds exactly the same opinions.
The Remarkable Rocket

The well-bred contradict other people. The wise contradict themselves.
Phrases and Philosophies for the Use of the Young

It is only the intellectually lost who can argue.
The Picture of Dorian Gray

A man who allows himself to be convinced by an argument is a thoroughly unreasonable person
An Ideal Husband

I dislike arguments of any kind. They are always vulgar,
and often convincing.
The Importance of Being Earnest

The Aristocracy
There is always more brass than brains in an aristocracy.
Vera, or The Nihilists

The Peerage is the one book a young man about town
should know thoroughly and it is the best thing in fiction
the English have ever done.
A Woman of No Importance

Art
There are two ways of disliking art . . . One is to dislike
it. The other is to like it rationally.
The Critic as Artist

All art is immoral. For emotion for the sake of emotion
is the aim of art, and emotion for the sake of action is the
aim of life.
The Critic as Artist

It is only an auctioneer who can equally and impartially admire all schools of Art
The Critic as Artist

Art is the most intense mode of Individualism that the world has known.
The Soul of Man Under Socialism

Art finds her own perfection within, and not outside of, herself. She is not to be judged by any external standards of resemblance. She is a veil, rather than a mirror. She has flowers that no forests know of, birds that no wood-land possess. She makes and unmakes many worlds, and can draw the moon from heaven with a scarlet thread. Hers are the forms more real than living man, and hers the great archetypes of which things that have existence are but unfinished copies. Nature has, in her eyes, no law, no uniformity.
The Decay of Lying

The telling of beautiful untrue things, is the proper aim of Art.

> *The Decay of Lying*

We can forgive a man for making a useful thing as long as he does not admire it.   The only excuse or making a useless thing is that one admires it intensely. All art is quite useless.

> *The Picture of Dorian Gray*

Art and Nature
One touch of Nature may make the whole world kin, but two touches of Nature will destroy any work of Art.

> *The Decay of Lying*

What Art really reveals to us is Nature's lack of design, her curious crudities, her extraordinary monotony, her absolutely unfinished condition. Nature has good intentions, of course, but as Aristotle once said, she cannot carry them out.

> *The Decay of Lying*

The Artist
She is like most artists; she is all style without any sincerity.

> *The Nightingale and the Rose*

The true artist is a man who believes absolutely in himself, because he is absolutely himself.

> *The Soul of Man Under Socialism*

To call an artist morbid because he deals with morbidity as his subject-matter is as silly as if one called Shakespeare mad because he wrote *King Lear*.

> *The Soul of Man Under Socialism*

No great artist ever sees things as they really are. If he did he would cease to be an artist.

The Decay of Lying

Bad artists always admire each other's work. They call it being large-minded and free from prejudice. But a truly great artist cannot conceive of life being shown, or beauty fashioned, under any conditions other than those he has selected.

The Critic as Artist

Bachelors

Nowadays all the married men are like bachelors, and all the bachelors like married men.

The Picture of Dorian Gray

Bachelors are not fashionable any more. They are a damaged lot. Too much is known about them.

An Ideal Husband

By persistently remaining single, a man converts himself into a permanent public temptation. Men should be more careful; this very celibacy leads weaker vessels astray.

The Importance of Being Earnest

Beauty

To be perfectly proportioned is a rare thing in an age when so many women are either over life-size or insignificant.

Lord Arthur Savile's Crime

All beautiful things belong to the same age.

Pen, Pencil and Poison

Beauty is a form of Genius – is higher, indeed, than Genius as it needs no explanation.
The Picture of Dorian Gray

Beauty, real beauty, ends where an intellectual expression begins. Intellect is in itself a mode of exaggeration and destroys the harmony of any face. The moment one sits down to think, one becomes all nose, or all forehead, or something horrid.
The Picture of Dorian Gray

I think that it is better to be beautiful than to be good. But on the other hand no one is more ready than I am to acknowledge that it is better to be good than to be ugly.
The Picture of Dorian Gray

Those who find ugly meanings in beautiful things are corrupt without being charming. That is a fault.
Those who find beautiful meanings in beautiful things are the cultivated. For these there is hope.
They are the elect to whom beautiful things mean only Beauty.
The Picture of Dorian Gray

Even men of the noblest possible moral character are extremely susceptible to the influence of the physical charms of others.
The Importance of Being Earnest

Behaviour
If we lived long enough to see the results of our actions it may be that those who call themselves good would be sickened with a dull remorse, and those whom the world calls evil stirred by a noble joy.
The Critic as Artist

It is quite remarkable how one good action always breeds another.
The Devoted Friend

Any preoccupation with ideas of what is right or wrong in conduct shows an arrested intellectual development.
Phrases and Philosophies for the Use of the Young

One should always be a little improbable.
Phrases and Philosophies for the Use of the Young

The basis of every scandal is an immoral certainty.
The Picture of Dorian Gray

Whenever a man does a thoroughly stupid thing, it is always from the noblest of motives.
The Picture of Dorian Gray

The one advantage of playing with fire is that one never gets even singed. It is the people who don't know how to play with it who get burned up.
A Woman of No Importance

To be natural is such a very difficult pose to keep up.
　　An Ideal Husband

It is always nice to be expected and not to arrive.
　　An Ideal Husband

One should always play fairly – when one has the winning cards.
　　An Ideal Husband

Being natural is simply a pose, and the most irritating pose I know.
　　The Picture of Dorian Gray

Belief
Man can believe the impossible, but man can never believe the improbable.
　　The Decay of Lying

As for believing things, I can believe anything, provided that it is quite incredible.
　　The Picture of Dorian Gray

Biography
Every great man nowadays has his disciples and it is always Judas who writes the biography.
　　The Critic as Artist

The Bore
One should never take sides in anything. Taking sides is the beginning of sincerity and earnestness follows shortly afterwards, and the human being becomes a bore.
　　A Woman of No Importance

Breakfast
Only dull people are brilliant at breakfast.
  An Ideal Husband

Character
It is only the superficial qualities that last. Man's deeper nature is soon found out.
  Phrases and Philosophies for the Use of the Young

A man cannot always be estimated by what he does. He may keep the law, and yet be worthless. He may break the law and yet be fine.
  The Soul of Man Under Socialism

A bad man is the sort of man who admires innocence, and a bad woman is the sort of woman a man never gets tired of.
  A Woman of No Importance

He has one of those terribly weak natures that are not susceptible to influence.
  An Ideal Husband

Charm
I don't know that women are always rewarded for being charming. I think they are usually punished for it!
  An Ideal Husband

When men give up saying what is charming, they give up thinking what is charming.
  Lady Windermere's Fan

Children
A family is a terrible encumbrance, especially when one is not married.
Vera, or The Nihilists

Children begin by loving their parents. After a time they judge them. Rarely, if ever do they forgive them.
A Woman of No Importance

Few parents nowadays pay any regard to what their children say to them. The old-fashioned respect for the young is fast dying.
The Importance of Being Earnest

Chopin
After playing Chopin, I feel as if I had been weeping over sins that I had never committed, and mourning over tragedies that were not my own. Music always seems to me to produce that effect. It creates for one a past of which one has been ignorant and fills one with a sense of sorrows that have been hidden from one's tears.
The Critic as Artist

LORD HENRY: You must play Chopin to me. The man with whom my wife ran away played Chopin exquisitely.
The Picture of Dorian Gray

Civilization
Savages seem to have quite the same views as cultured people on almost all subjects. They are excessively advanced.
A Woman of No Importance

Clever People
You can't go anywhere without meeting clever people. The thing has become an absolute public nuisance. I wish to goodness we had a few fools left.
The Importance of Being Earnest

Common Sense
Nowadays most people die of a sort of creeping common sense, and discover when it is too late that the only things one never regrets are one's mistakes.
The Picture of Dorian Gray

No woman, plain or pretty, has any common sense at all. Common sense is the privilege of our sex.
An Ideal Husband

Compliments
Nowadays we are all of us so hard up, that the only pleasant things to pay *are* compliments. They're the only things we *can* pay.
Lady Windermere's Fan

An acquaintance that begins with a compliment is sure to develop into a real friendship. It starts in the right manner.
An Ideal Husband

Conceit
I don't at all like knowing what people say of me behind my back. It makes one far too conceited.
An Ideal Husband

Confession
It is the confession, not the priest that gives us absolution.
The Picture of Dorian Gray

Conscience
Conscience and cowardice are really the same things. Conscience is the trade-name of the firm.
The Picture of Dorian Gray

Conversation
'There is no good talking to him,' said a Dragonfly, who was sitting on the top of a large brown bulrush; 'no good at all, for he has gone away.'

'Well, that is his loss, not mine,' answered the Rocket. 'I am not going to stop talking to him merely because he pays no attention. I like hearing myself talk. It is one of my greatest pleasures. I often have long conversations all by myself, and I am so clever that sometimes I don't understand a single word of what I am saying.'
The Remarkable Rocket

I like to do all the talking myself. It saves time and prevents arguments.

The Remarkable Rocket

I hate people who talk about themselves, as you do, when one wants to talk about oneself, as I do.

The Remarkable Rocket

He never said a brilliant or even an ill-natured thing in his life.

The Model Millionaire

That some change will take place before this century has drawn to its close we have no doubt whatsoever. Bored by the tedious and improving conversation of those who have neither the wit to exaggerate nor the genius to romance, tired of the intelligent person whose reminiscences are always based on memory, whose statements are invariably limited by probability, and who is at any time liable to be corroborated by the merest Philistine who happens to be present, Society sooner or later must return to is lost leader, the cultured and fascinating liar.

The Decay of Lying

Conversation should touch everything but should concentrate itself on nothing.

The Critic as Artist

When people talk to us about others they are usually dull. When they talk to us about themselves they are nearly always interesting, and if one could shut them up, when they become wearisome, as easily as one can shut up a book of which one has grown wearied, they would be perfect absolutely.

The Critic as Artist

28

Lots of people act well but very few people talk well, which shows that talking is much more the difficult thing of the two, and much the finer thing also.
The Devoted Friend

There is only one thing in the world worse than being talked about, and that it not being talked about.
The Picture of Dorian Gray

I like talking to a brick wall, it's the only thing in the world that never contradicts me.
Lady Windermere's Fan

MRS ALLONBY: You should certainly know Ernest, Lady Stutfield. It is only fair to tell you beforehand he has got no conversation at all.
LADY STUTFIELD: I adore silent men.
MRS ALLONBY: Oh, Ernest isn't silent. He talks the whole time. But he has got no conversation.
A Woman of No Importance

Everything you have said to-day seems to be excessively immoral. It has been most interesting, listening to you.
A Woman of No Importance

A man who can dominate a London dinner-table can dominate the world. The future belongs to the dandy. It is the exquisites who are going to rule.
A Woman of No Importance

The clever people never listen, and the stupid people never talk.
A Woman of No Importance

LORD CAVERSHAM: Do you always really understand
                          what you say, sir?
LORD GORING (*after some hesitation*):
                          Yes, father, if I listen attentively.
    An Ideal Husband

I usually say what I really think. A great mistake nowadays. It makes one so liable to be misunderstood.
    An Ideal Husband

Whenever people talk to me about the weather, I always feel certain that they mean something else.
    The Importance of Being Earnest

Criminals
Our criminals are, as a class, so absolutely uninteresting from any psychological point of view. They are not marvellous Macbeths and terrible Vautrins. They are merely what ordinary, respectable, commonplace people would be if they had not got enough to eat.
    The Soul of Man Under Socialism

The Critic
The first duty of an art critic is to hold his tongue at all times, and upon all subjects.
    The English Renaissance of Art

I am always amused by the silly vanity of those writers and artists of our day who seem to imagine that the primary function of the critics is to chatter about their second-rate work.
    The Critic as Artist

ERNEST: Simply this: that in the best days of art there were no art-critics.

GILBERT: I seem to have heard that observation before, Ernest. It has all the vitality of error and all the tediousness of an old friend.

The Critic as Artist

Cynicism
You never say a moral thing, and you never do a wrong thing. Your cynicism is simply a pose.

The Picture of Dorian Gray

A cynic is a man who knows the price of everything and the value of nothing.

Lady Windermere's Fan

Death
Death is not a God. He is only the servant of the gods.

La Sainte Courtisane

Democracy
High hopes were once formed of democracy; but democracy means simply the bludgeoning of the people by the people for the people.

The Soul of Man Under Socialism

Destiny
In her dealings with man Destiny never closes her accounts.

The Picture of Dorian Gray

Diary
I never travel without my diary. One should always have something sensational to read in the train.
The Importance of Being Earnest

Diplomacy
To make a good salad is to be a brilliant diplomatist – the problem is entirely the same in both cases. To know exactly how much oil one must put with one's vinegar.
Vera, or The Nihilists

She was made to be an ambassador's wife. She certainly has a wonderful faculty of remembering people's names, and forgetting their faces.
A Woman of No Importance

Disapproval
I never approve, or disapprove, of anything now. It is an absurd attitude to take towards life. We are not sent into the world to air our moral Prejudices. I never take any notice of what common people say, and I never interfere with what charming people do.
The Picture of Dorian Gray

Domesticity
As for domesticity, it ages one rapidly, and distracts one's mind from higher things.
The Remarkable Rocket

I have often observed that in married households the champagne is rarely of a first-rate brand.
The Importance of Being Earnest

The Dreamer
Yes: I am a dreamer. For a dreamer is one who can only find his way by moonlight, and his punishment is that he sees the dawn before the rest of the world.
The Critic as Artist

Dullness
Dullness is the coming-of-age of seriousness.
Phrases and Philosophies for the Use of the Young

Duty
The first duty in life is to be as artificial as possible. What the second duty is no one has yet discovered.
Phrases and Philosophies for the Use of the Young

Duty is what one expects from others, it is not what one does oneself.
A Woman of No Importance

My duty is a thing I never do, on principle.
An Ideal Husband

What between the duties expected of one during one's lifetime, and the duties exacted from one after one's death, land has ceased to be either a profit or a pleasure.
The Importance of Being Earnest

Education
The mind of a thoroughly well-informed man is a dreadful thing. It is like a bric-a-brac shop, all monsters and dust, with everything priced above its proper value.
The Picture of Dorian Gray

Education is an admirable thing, but it is well to remember from time to time that nothing that is worth knowing can be taught.

The Critic as Artist

To have been well brought up is a great drawback nowadays. It shuts one out from so much.

A Woman of No Importance

LADY BASILDON: Ah! I hate being educated!
MRS MARCHMONT: So do I. It puts one almost on a level with the commercial classes.

An Ideal Husband

In England, at any rate, education produces no effect whatsoever. If it did, it would prove a serious danger to the upper classes, and would probably lead to acts of violence in Grosvenor Square.
The Importance of Being Earnest

Egotism
Egotism itself, which is so necessary to a proper sense of human dignity, is entirely the result of an indoor life.
The Decay of Lying

Eloquence
She doesn't care much for eloquence in others. She thinks it a little loud.
An Ideal Husband

Emotion
Emotion for the sake of emotion is the aim of art, and emotion for the sake of action is the aim of life.
The Critic as Artist

It is only shallow people who require years to get rid of an emotion. A man who is master of himself, can end a sorrow as easily as he can invent a pleasure.
The Picture of Dorian Gray

The secret of life is never to have an emotion that is unbecoming.
A Woman of No Importance

Moods don't last. It is their chief charm.
A Woman of No Importance

A woman's life revolves in curves of emotion. It is upon lines of intellect that a man's life progresses.
An Ideal Husband

I cannot repeat an emotion. No one can, except sentimentalists.
The Picture of Dorian Gray

England and the English
England will never be civilized until she has added Utopia to her dominions.
The Critic as Artist

Thinking is the most unhealthy thing in the world, and people die of it just as they die of any other disease. Fortunately, in England at any rate, thought is not catching. Our splendid physique as a people is entirely due to our national stupidity.
The Decay of Lying

I don't think England should be represented abroad by an unmarried man . . . . It might lead to complications.
A Woman of No Importance

A Typical Englishman, always dull and usually violent.
An Ideal Husband

The English can't stand a man who is always saying he is right, but they are very fond of a man who admits he has been in the wrong.
An Ideal Husband

The English think that a cheque book can solve every problem in life.
An Ideal Husband

The English and the Irish
If one could only teach the English how to talk, and the Irish how to listen, society here would be quite civilised.
An Ideal Husband

Epigrams
He would stab his best friend for the sake of writing an epigram on his tombstone.
Vera, or The Nihilists

One dagger will do more than a hundred epigrams.
Vera, or The Nihilists

You would sacrifice anybody, Harry, for the sake of an epigram.
The Picture of Dorian Gray

Examinations
In examinations the foolish ask questions that the wise cannot answer.
Phrases and Philosophies for the Use of the Young

Example
Really, if the lower orders don't set us a good example, what on earth is the use of them?
The Importance of Being Earnest

Excuse
I am prevented from coming in consequence of a subsequent engagement.
The Picture of Dorian Gray

Exhilaration
A chase after a beautiful woman is always exciting.
Vera, or The Nihilists

Experience
Personal experience is a most vicious and limited circle.
The Decay of Lying

Experience is the name everyone gives to their mistakes.
Lady Windermere's Fan

Twenty years of romance make a woman look like a ruin;
but twenty years of marriage make her look like a public
building.
A Woman of No Importance

Fashion
Nothing is so dangerous as
being too modern. One is
apt to grow old-fashioned
quite suddenly.
An Ideal Husband

Fashion is what one
wears oneself. What is
unfashionable is what
other people wear.
An Ideal Husband

One should never give
a woman anything she
can't wear in the
evening.
An Ideal Husband

To be pretty is the best fashion there is, and the only fashion that England succeeds in setting.
An Ideal Husband

Fathers
Fathers should neither be seen nor heard. That is the only proper basis for family life.
An Ideal Husband

Flattery
LADY WINDERMERE: I don't like compliments and I don't see why a man should think he is pleasing a woman enormously when he says to her a whole heap of things that he doesn't mean.
Lady Windermere's Fan

Flirtation
A woman will flirt with anybody in the world as long as other people are looking on.
The Picture of Dorian Gray

The only way to behave to a woman is to make love to her, if she is pretty, and to someone else, if she is plain.
The Importance of Being Earnest

The amount of women in London who flirt with their own husbands is perfectly scandalous. It looks so bad. It is simply washing one's clean linen in public.
The Importance of Being Earnest

Food and Drink
It is very poor consolation to be told that the man who has given one a bad dinner, or poor wine, is irreproachable in private life. Even the cardinal virtues cannot atone for half-cold entrées.
The Picture of Dorian Gray

When I am in really great trouble, as anyone who knows me intimately will tell you, I refuse everything except food and drink.
The Importance of Being Earnest

Fortune Telling
I think everyone should have their hands told once a month so as to know what not to do.
Lord Arthur Savile's Crime

Forgiveness
Women are not meant to judge us, but to forgive us when we need forgiveness. Pardon, not punishment, is their mission.
An Ideal Husband

Fox-hunting
One knows so well the popular idea of health. The English country-gentleman galloping after a fox – the unspeakable in full pursuit of the uneatable.
A Woman of No Importance

Friends
I always like to know everything about my new friends, and nothing about my old ones.
The Picture of Dorian Gray

One has a right to judge a man by the effect he has over his friends.
> *The Picture of Dorian Gray*

I dare say that if I knew him I should not be his friend at all. It is a very dangerous thing to know one's friends.
> *The Remarkable Rocket*

The absence of old friends one can endure with equanimity. But even a momentary separation from anyone to whom one has just been introduced is almost unbearable.
> *The Importance of Being Earnest*

Friendship
Anybody can sympathize with the sufferings of a friend, but it requires a very fine nature to sympathize with a friend's success.
> *The Soul of Man Under Socialism*

What is the good of friendship if one cannot say exactly what one means.
> *The Devoted Friend*

I think that generosity is the essence of friendship.
> *The Devoted Friend*

Between men and women there is no friendship possible. There is passion, enmity, worship, love, but no friendship.
> *Lady Windermere's Fan*

The Future
But the past is of no importance. The present is of no importance. It is with the future that we have to deal. For the past is what man should not have been. The present is what man ought not to be. The future is what artists are.
The Soul of Man Under Socialism

Genius
The public is wonderfully tolerant. It forgives everything except genius.
The Critic as Artist

Not being a genius, he had no enemies.
Lord Arthur Savile's Crime

Geniuses . . . are always talking about themselves, when I want them to be thinking about me.
An Ideal Husband

I like looking at geniuses, and listening to beautiful people.
An Ideal Husband

Gentlemen
If a man is a gentleman, he knows quite enough, and if he is not a gentleman, whatever he knows is bad for him.
The Picture of Dorian Gray

One of Nature's gentlemen, the worst type of gentleman I know.
Lady Windermere's Fan

Good and Bad
It is absurd to divide people into good and bad. People are either charming or tedious.
Lady Windermere's Fan

Good Intentions
It is always with the best intentions that the worst work is done.
The Critic as Artist

Good Taste
Good taste is the excuse I've always given for leading such a bad life.
The Importance of Being Earnest

Good Temper
MRS ALLONBY: Nothing is so aggravating as calmness. There is something positively brutal about the good temper of the most modern men. I wonder we women stand it as well as we do.
A Woman of No Importance

Gossip
It is perfectly monstrous the way people go about, nowadays, saying things against one behind one's back that are absolutely and entirely true.
A Woman of No Importance

Grande Passion
A really *grande passion* is comparatively rare nowadays. It is the privilege of people who have nothing to do. That is the one use of the idle classes in a country.
A Woman of No Importance

Happiness
When we are happy we are always good but when we are good we are not always happy.
The Picture of Dorian Gray

Heroes
Formerly we used to canonize our heroes. The modern method is to vulgarize them. Cheap editions of great books may be delightful, but cheap editions of great men are absolutely detestable.
The Critic as Artist

History
The one duty we owe to history is to rewrite it.
The Critic as Artist

Anybody can make history. Only a great man can write it.
The Critic as Artist

Hospitality
For a house lacking a host is but an empty thing and void of honour.
A Florentine Tragedy

Human Nature
The more one analyses people, the more all reasons for analysis disappear. Sooner or later one comes to that dreadful universal thing called human nature.
The Decay of Lying

Husbands
The husbands of very beautiful women belong to the criminal classes.
The Picture of Dorian Gray

Men are horribly tedious when they are good husbands, and abominably conceited when they are not.
    A Woman of No Importance

Plain women are always jealous of their husbands. Beautiful women never have time. They are always so occupied in being jealous of other people's husbands.
    A Woman of No Importance

People are either hunting for husbands, or hiding from them.
    An Ideal Husband

Idleness
The condition of perfection is idleness; the aim of perfection is youth.
    Phrases and Philosophies for the Use of the Young

Let me say to you now that to do nothing at all is the most difficult thing in the world, the most difficult, and the most intellectual.
    The Critic as Artist

He rides in the Row at ten o'clock in the morning, goes to the Opera three times a week, changes his clothes at least five times a day, and dines out every night of the season. You don't call that leading an idle life, do you?
    An Ideal Husband

Ignorance
Ignorance is like a delicate exotic fruit; touch it and the bloom is gone.
    The Importance of Being Earnest

Illness
Illness of any kind is hardly a thing to be encouraged in
others. Health is the primary duty of life.
Lady Windermere's Fan

Industry
Industry is the root of all ugliness.
Phrases and Philosophies for the Use of the Young

Infidelity
There's no pleasure in taking in a husband who never
sees anything.
The Picture of Dorian Gray

When a woman finds out about her husband she either
becomes dreadfully dowdy, or wears very smart bonnets
that some other woman's husband has to pay for.
The Picture of Dorian Gray

Those who are faithful know only the trivial side of love:
it is the faithless who know love's tragedies.
The Picture of Dorian Gray

Young men want to be faithful and are not; old men want
to be faithless and cannot.
The Picture of Dorian Gray

Influence
There is no such thing as a good influence. All influence
is immoral – immoral from the scientific point of view.
The Picture of Dorian Gray

All influence is bad, but a good influence is the worst in
the world.
A Woman of No Importance

Innocence
Nothing looks so like innocence as an indiscretion.
Lord Arthur Savile's Crime

What have women who have not sinned to do with me,
or I with them? We do not understand each other.
A Woman of No Importance

Insincerity
What people call insincerity is simply a method by which
we can multiply our personalities.
The Critic as Artist

Intellect
Intellect is in itself a mode of exaggeration, and destroys
the harmony of any face. The moment one sits down to
think, one becomes all nose, or all forehead, or something horrid.
The Picture of Dorian Gray

Nothing refines but the intellect.
A Woman of No Importance

Kindness
One can always be kind to people
about whom one cares nothing.
The Picture of Dorian Gray

A Kiss
A kiss may ruin a human life.
*A Woman of No
Importance*

Labour
It is mentally and morally injurious to a man to do anything in which he does not find pleasure, and many forms
of labour are quite pleasureless activities and should be
regarded as such . . . . Man is made for something better
than disturbing dirt. All work of that kind should be
done by a machine.
The Soul of Man Under Socialism

Laughter
Laughter is not at all a bad beginning for a friendship,
and it is far the best ending for one.
The Picture of Dorian Gray

Leisure
Cultivated leisure is the aim of man.
The Soul of Man Under Socialism

Life
Life is much too important a thing ever to talk seriously
about it.
Vera, or The Nihilists

There are few things easier than to live badly and to die
well.
Vera, or The Nihilists

One can live for years sometimes without living at all,
and then all life comes crowding into one single hour.
Vera, or The Nihilists

Nothing that actually occurs is of the smallest importance.
Phrases and Philosophies for the Use of the Young

To live is the rarest thing in the world. Most people exist, that is all.
The Soul of Man Under Socialism

Nowadays it is only the unreadable that occurs.
A Woman of No Importance

To become a spectator of one's own life is to escape the suffering of life.
The Picture of Dorian Gray

We live in an age that reads too much to be wise, and thinks too much to be beautiful.
The Picture of Dorian Gray

I love acting. It is so much more real than life.
The Picture of Dorian Gray

We can have in life but one great experience at best, and the secret of life is to reproduce that experience as often as possible.
The Picture of Dorian Gray

In this world there are only two tragedies. One is not getting what one wants and the other is getting it.
Lady Windermere's Fan

The Book of Life begins with a man and woman in a garden. It ends with Revelations.
A Woman of No Importance

I hope you don't think you have exhausted life . . . . When a man says that, one knows that life has exhausted him.
A Woman of No Importance

Life . . . is simply a *mauvais quart d'heure* made up of exquisite moments.
A Woman of No Importance

Life is never fair . . . And perhaps it is a good thing for most of us that it is not.
An Ideal Husband

Literature
If one cannot enjoy reading a book over and over again, there is no use in reading it at all.
The Decay of Living

To know the vintage and quality of a wine one need not drink the whole cask. It must be perfectly easy in half an hour to say whether a book is worth anything or worth nothing. Ten minutes are really sufficient, if one has the instinct for form. Who wants to wade through a dull volume? One tastes it, and that is quite enough.
The Critic as Artist

Journalism is unreadable, and literature is not read.
The Critic as Artist

There is no such thing as a moral or an immoral book. Books are well written or badly written. That is all.
The Picture of Dorian Gray

I hate vulgar realism in literature. The man who could call a spade a spade should be compelled to use one. It is the only thing he is fit for.
The Picture of Dorian Gray

Love
Love is an illusion.
The Picture of Dorian Gray

Any place you love is the world to you . . . but love is not fashionable any more, the poets have killed it. They wrote so much about it that nobody believed them, and I am not surprised. True love suffers, and is silent.
The Remarkable Rocket

They do not sin at all
Who sin for love.
The Duchess of Padua

What a silly thing love is! It is not half as useful as logic, for it does not prove anything and it is always telling one things that are not going to happen, and making one believe things that are not true.

The Nightingale and the Rose

DUCHESS OF MONMOUTH: We women, as someone says, love with our ears, just as you men love with your eyes, if you ever love at all.

The Picture of Dorian Gray

A man can be happy with any woman as long as he does not love her.

The Picture of Dorian Gray

Not love at first sight, but love at the end of the season, which is so much more satisfactory.

Lady Windermere's Fan

Men always want to be a woman's first love. That is their clumsy vanity. Women have a more subtle instinct about things: What they like is to be a man's last romance.

A Woman of No Importance

Who, being loved, is poor?

A Woman of No Importance

It is not the perfect but the imperfect who have need of love.

An Ideal Husband

There is always something ridiculous about the emotions of people whom one has ceased to love.
The Picture of Dorian Gray

It is love, and not German philosophy, that is the true explanation of this world, whatever may be the explanation of the next.
An Ideal Husband

Marriage
I am not in favour of long engagements. They give people the opportunity of finding out each other's character before marriage, which I think is never advisable.
The Importance of Being Earnest

Once a week is quite enough to propose to anyone, and it should always be done in a manner that attracts some attention.
An Ideal Husband

The proper basis for marriage is mutual misunderstanding.
Lord Arthur Savile's Crime

Men marry because they are tired; women because they are curious; both are disappointed.
The Picture of Dorian Gray

The one charm of marriage is that it makes a life of deception absolutely necessary for both parties.
The Picture of Dorian Gray

There's nothing in the world like the devotion of a married woman. It's a thing no married man knows anything about.

    Lady Windermere's Fan

The real drawback to marriage is that it makes one unselfish. And unselfish people are colourless.

    The Picture of Dorian Gray

Of course married life is merely a habit, a bad habit. But then one regrets the loss of even one's worst habits. Perhaps one regrets them the most. They are such an essential part of one's personality.
The Picture of Dorian Gray

When a woman marries again, it is because she detested her first husband. When a man marries again, it is because he adored his first wife. Women try their luck; men risk theirs.
The Picture of Dorian Gray

It is a curious thing about the game of marriage – the wives hold all the honours, and invariably lose the odd trick.
Lady Windermere's Fan

It's most dangerous nowadays for a husband to pay any attention to his wife in public. It always makes people think that he beats her when they're alone.
Lady Windermere's Fan

LORD AUGUSTUS: It is a great thing to come across a woman who thoroughly understands one.

DUMBY: It is an awfully dangerous thing. They always end by marrying one.
Lady Windermere's Fan

How marriage ruins a man! It's as demoralizing as cigarettes, and far more expensive.
Lady Windermere's Fan

LADY CAROLINE:	Women have become so highly educated . . . that nothing should surprise us nowadays, except happy marriages. They apparently are getting very rare.
MRS ALLONBY:	Oh, they're quite out of date.
LADY STUTFIELD:	Except amongst the middle classes, I have been told.
MRS ALLONBY:	How like the middle classes!

A Woman of No Importance

The happiness of a married man depends on the people he has not married.

A Woman of No Importance

How can a woman be expected to be happy with a man who insists on treating her as if she were a perfectly natural being.

A Woman of No Importance

Englishwomen conceal their feelings till after they are married. They show them then.

A Woman of No Importance

To elope is cowardly. It's running away from danger. And danger has become so rare in modern life.

A Woman of No Importance

If we men married the women we deserve we should have a very bad time of it.

An Ideal Husband

There is one thing worse than an absolutely loveless marriage. A marriage in which there is love, but on one side only.

> *An Ideal Husband*

In married life affection comes when people thoroughly dislike each other.

> *An Ideal Husband*

It is the growth of the moral sense in women that makes marriage such a hopeless one-sided institution.

> *An Ideal Husband*

LADY MARKBY: In my time . . . we were taught not to understand anything. That was the old system, and wonderfully interesting it was. I assure you that the amount of things I and my poor sister were taught not to understand was quite extraordinary. But modern women understand everything, I am told.

MRS CHEVELEY: Except their husbands. That is the one thing the modern woman never understands.

LADY MARKBY: And a very good thing too, dear, I dare say. It might break up many a happy home if they did.

> *An Ideal Husband*

In married life three is company and two is none.

> *The Importance of Being Earnest*

I have always been of the opinion that a man who desires to get married should know either everything or nothing.
The Importance of Being Earnest

The very essence of romance is uncertainty. If ever I get married, I'll certainly try to forget the fact.
The Importance of Being Earnest

Maturity

MRS ALLONBY: I delight in men over seventy, they always offer one the devotion of a lifetime.
A Woman of No Importance

When a man is old enough to do wrong he should be old enough to do right also.
A Woman of No Importance

Mediocrity

Indifference is the revenge the world takes on mediocrities.
Vera, or The Nihilists

Caricature is the tribute mediocrity pays to genius.
A LECTURE IN AMERICA

Every effect that one produces gives one an enemy. To be popular one must be a mediocrity.
The Picture of Dorian Gray

Memory
That awful memory of woman! What a fearful thing it is!
And what an utter intellectual stagnation it reveals!
One should absorb the colour of life, but one should
never remember its details. Details are always vulgar.
The Picture of Dorian Gray

No woman should have a memory. Memory in a woman
is the beginning of dowdiness.
A Woman of No Importance

Memory is the diary that we all carry about with us.
The Importance of Being Earnest

Men
Men become old, but they never become good.
Lady Windermere's Fan

MRS ALLONBY: The Ideal Man . . . he should always
say much more than he means, and
always mean much more than he says.
A Woman of No Importance

MRS ALLONBY: The Ideal Man . . . should never run
down other pretty women. That would
show he had no taste or make one
suspect that he had too much.
A Woman of No Importance

CECILY: A man who is much talked about is always
attractive. One feels there must be something in him, after all.
The Importance of Being Earnest

Men and Women – the difference
Women are a decorative sex. They never have anything
to say, but they say it charmingly. Women represent the
triumph of matter over mind, just as men represent the
triumph of mind over morals.
 The Picture of Dorian Gray

Women know life too late. That is the difference
between men and women.
 A Woman of No Importance

I like men who have a future and women who have a
past.
 The Picture of Dorian Gray

 How hard good women are!
 How weak bad men are!
  Lady Windermere's Fan

GERALD: It is very difficult to under-
       stand women, is it not?
LORD ILLINGWORTH: You should never try to under-
       stand them. Women are pic-
       tures. Men are problems.
 A Woman of No Importance

MRS CHIEVELEY: The strength of women comes from
      the fact that psychology cannot
      explain us. Men can be analysed
      and women . . . merely adored.
 An Ideal Husband

Women are never disarmed by compliments. Men always are. That is the difference between the sexes.
An Ideal Husband

Moderation
Moderation is a fatal thing. Enough is as bad as a meal. More than enough is as good as a feast.
The Picture of Dorian Gray

Moderation is a fatal thing. Nothing succeeds like excess.
A Woman of No Importance

Modern Art
The best that one can say of most modern creative art is that it is just a little less vulgar than reality.
The Critic as Artist

Modern pictures are, no doubt, delightful to look at. At least, some of them are. But they are quite impossible to live with; they are too clever, too assertive, too intellectual. Their meaning is too obvious, and their method too clearly defined. One exhausts what they have to say in a very short time, and then they become as tedious as one's relations.
The Critic as Artist

Most of our modern portrait painters are doomed to oblivion. They never paint what they see. They paint what the public sees, and the public never sees anything.
The Decay of Lying

Money
It is better to have a permanent income than to be fascinating.
The Model Millionaire

There is only one class in the community that thinks more about money than the rich, and that is the poor. The poor can think of nothing else.
The Soul of Man Under Socialism

It is only by not paying one's bills that one can hope to live in the memory of the commercial classes.
Phrases and Philosophies for the Use of the Young

Credit is the capital of a younger son.
The Picture of Dorian Gray

Young people, nowadays, imagine that money is everything, and when they grow older they know it.
The Picture of Dorian Gray

I don't want money. It is only people who pay their bills who want that, and I never pay mine.
The Picture of Dorian Gray

Morality
Modern morality consists in accepting the standard of one's age. I consider that for any man of culture to accept the standard of his age is a form of the grossest immorality.
The Picture of Dorian Gray

Women are always on the side of morality, public and private.
A Woman of No Importance

Morality is simply the attitude we adopt to people whom we personally dislike.
An Ideal Husband

Moralizers
A man who moralizes is usually a hypocrite, and a woman who moralizes is invariably plain.
Lady Windermere's Fan

Mothers
A mother's love is very touching, of course, but it is often curiously selfish. I mean, there is a good deal of selfishness in it.
A Woman of No Importance

I should imagine that most mothers don't quite understand their sons.
A Woman of No Importance

I was influenced by my mother. Every man is when he is young.
A Woman of No Importance

All women become like their mothers. That is their tragedy. No man does. That's his.
The Importance of Being Earnest

Murder
Murder is always a mistake . . . . One should never do anything that one cannot talk about after dinner.
The Picture of Dorian Gray

Music
Music makes one feel so romantic – at least it always got on one's nerves – which is the same thing nowadays.
A Woman of No Importance

I don't play accurately – anyone can play accurately – but I play with wonderful expression. As far as the piano is concerned, sentiment is my *forte*. I keep science for life.
The Importance of Being Earnest

If one plays good music people don't listen, and if one plays bad music people don't talk.
The Importance of Being Earnest

Musical People
Musical people are so absurdly unreasonable. They always want one to be perfectly dumb at the very

64

moment when one is longing to be absolutely deaf.
An Ideal Husband

Mysteries
Nowadays we have so few mysteries left to us that we
cannot afford to part with one of them.
The Critic as Artist

Novels
The ancient historians gave us delightful fiction in the
form of fact; the modern novelist presents us with dull
facts under the guise of fiction.
The Decay of Lying

I quite admit that modern novels have many good points.
All I insist on is that, as a class, they are quite unread-
able.
The Decay of Lying

Anybody can write a three-volumed novel. It merely
requires a complete ignorance of both life and literature.
The Critic as Artist

The popular novel that the public call healthy is always a thoroughly unhealthy production; and what the public call an unhealthy novel is always a beautiful and healthy work of art.

> *The Soul of Man Under Socialism*

Omens

As for omens, there is no such thing as an omen. Destiny does not send us heralds. She is too wise or too cruel for that.

> *The Picture of Dorian Gray*

Parents

Why will parents always appear at the wrong time? Some extraordinary mistake in nature, I suppose.

> *An Ideal Husband*

To lose one parent . . . may be regarded as a misfortune; to lose both looks like carelessness.

> *The Importance of Being Earnest*

Passion

I might mimic a passion that I do not feel, but I cannot mimic one that burns one like fire.

> *The Picture of Dorian Gray*

It is said that passion makes one think in a circle.

> *The Picture of Dorian Gray*

Nothing is serious except passion. The intellect is not a serious thing, and never has been. It is an instrument on which one plays, that is all.

> *A Woman of No Importance*

The Past
The one charm of the past is that it is past. But women never know when the curtain has fallen.
The Picture of Dorian Gray

What other people call one's past has, no doubt, everything to do with them, but absolutely nothing to do with oneself. The man who regards his past is a man who deserves to have no future to look forward to.
The Critic as Artist

People
There are only two kinds of people who are really fascinating – people who know absolutely everything and people who know absolutely nothing.
The Picture of Dorian Gray

I like persons better than principles and I like persons with no principles better than anything else in the world.
The Picture of Dorian Gray

I'm sure I don't know half the people who come to my house. Indeed, from all I hear, I shouldn't like to.
An Ideal Husband

Philanthropy
Philanthropy seems to me to have become simply the refuge of people who wish to annoy their fellow creatures.
An Ideal Husband

Plain Women
I don't mind plan women being Puritans. It is the only excuse they have for being plain.
A Woman of No Importance

Platitudes
In modern life nothing produces such an effect as a good platitude. It makes the whole world kin.
An Ideal Husband

Pleasure
I adore simple pleasures, they are the last refuge of the complex.
A Woman of No Importance

LORD GORING:	I love talking about nothing, father. It is the only thing I know anything about.
LORD CAVERSHAM:	You seem to me to be living entirely for pleasure.
LORD GORING:	What else is there to live for, Father? Nothing ages like happiness.

An Ideal Husband

LADY BRACKNELL:	I had some crumpets with Lady Harbury, who seems to me to be living entirely for pleasure now.
ALGERNON:	I hear her hair has turned quite gold from grief.

The Importance of Being Earnest

My duty as a gentleman has never interfered with my pleasures in the smallest degree.
The Importance of Being Earnest

An inordinate passion for pleasure is the secret of remaining young.
Lord Arthur Savile's Crime

'I have never searched for happiness. Who wants happiness? I have searched for pleasure.'
'And found it, Mr Gray?'
'Often. Too often.'
The Picture of Dorian Gray

No civilized man ever regrets a pleasure, and no uncivilized man ever knows what a pleasure is.
The Picture of Dorian Gray

Poetry
All fine imaginative work is self-conscious and deliberate. No poet sings because he must sing. At least no great poet does. A great poet sings because he chooses to sing.
The Critic as Artist

All bad poetry springs from genuine feeling. To be natural is to be obvious, and to be obvious is to be inartistic.
The Critic as Artist

A great poet, a really great poet, is the most unpoetical of creatures. But inferior poets are absolutely fascinating. The worse their rhymes the more picturesque they look. The mere fact of having published a book of second-rate sonnets makes a man quite irresistible. He lives the poetry he cannot write. The others write the poetry that they dare not realize.
The Picture of Dorian Gray

Politics and Politicians
There is hardly a single person in the House of Commons worth painting; though many of them would be better for a little whitewashing.
The Picture of Dorian Gray

He thinks like a Tory, and talks like a Radical, and that's so important nowadays.
Lady Windermere's Fan

KELVIN: May I ask, Lord Illingworth, if you regard the House of Lords as a better institution than the House of Commons?

LORD ILLINGWORTH: A much better institution of course. We in the House of Lords are never in touch with public opinion. That makes us a civilized body.

A Woman of No Importance

KELVIN: You cannot deny that the House of Commons has always shown great sympathy with the suffering of the poor.

LORD ILLINGWORTH: That is its special vice. That is the special vice of the age. One should sympathize with the joy, the beauty, the colour of life. The less said about life's sores the better.

A Woman of No Importance

MABEL CHILTERN: Oh! I hope you are not going to leave me all alone with Lord Goring? Especially at such an early hour in the day.

LORD CAVERSHAM: I am afraid I can't take him with me to Downing Street. It is not the Prime Minister's day for seeing the unemployed.

An Ideal Husband

Only people who look dull ever get into the House of Commons, and only people who are dull ever succeed there.

An Ideal Husband

Picturesqueness cannot survive the House of Commons.
An Ideal Husband

In England a man who can't talk morality twice a week to a large, popular, immoral audience is quite over as a serious politician.
An Ideal Husband

The Poor
Sometimes the poor are praised for being thrifty. But to recommend thrift to the poor is both grotesque and insulting. It is like advising a man who is starving to eat less.
The Soul of Man Under Socialism

As for the virtuous poor, one can pity them, of course, but one cannot possibly admire them.
The Soul of Man Under Socialism

I should fancy that the real tragedy of the poor is that they can afford nothing but self-denial.
The Picture of Dorian Gray

Portraits
The only portraits in which one believes are portraits where there is very little of the sitter and a very great deal of the artist.
The Decay of Lying

The Press
To have a style so gorgeous that it conceals the subject is one of the highest achievements of an important and much admired school of Fleet Street leader-writers.
Pen, Pencil and Poison

Lying for the sake of a monthly salary is, of course, well known in Fleet Street, and the profession of a political leader-writer is not without advantages. But it is said to be a somewhat dull occupation, and it certainly does not lead to much beyond a kind of ostentatious obscurity.

The Decay of Lying

Modern journalism, by giving us the opinions of the uneducated, keeps us in touch with the ignorance of the community.

The Critic as Artist

With regard to modern journalists, they always apologize to one in private for what they have written against one in public.

The Soul of Man Under Socialism

The public have an insatiable curiosity to know everything, except what is worth knowing. Journalism, conscious of this, and having tradesman-like habits, supplies their demands. In centuries before ours the public nailed the ears of journalists to the pump. That was quite hideous. In this century journalists have nailed their own ears to the keyhole.

The Soul of Man Under Socialism

Somebody – was it Burke? – called journalism the fourth estate. That was true at the time, no doubt. But at the present moment it really is the only estate. It has eaten up the other three. The Lords Temporal say nothing, the Lords Spiritual have nothing to say, and the House of Commons has nothing to say and says it. We are dominated by Journalism. In America the President reigns for four years, and Journalism goes on for ever and ever.

The Soul of Man Under Socialism

VICOMTE DE NANJAC: I read all your English newspapers. I find them so amusing.

LORD GORING: Then, my dear Nanjac, you must certainly read between the lines.

An Ideal Husband

MRS CHEVELEY: I am quite looking forward to meeting your clever husband, Lady Chiltern . . . . they actually succeed in spelling his name right in the newspapers. That in itself is fame, on the Continent.

An Ideal Husband

Principles
I don't like principles . . . I prefer prejudices.
An Ideal Husband

Progress
'Comfort' said Mr Podgers, 'and modern improvements and hot water laid on in every bedroom. Your Grace is quite right. Comfort is the only thing our civilization can give us.'
Lord Arthur Savile's Crime

Discontent is the first step in the progress of a man or a nation.
A Woman of No Importance

The Public
The public have an insatiable curiosity to know everything, except what is worth knowing.
The Soul of Man Under Socialism

The private lives of men and women should not be told to the public. The public have nothing to do with them at all.
> *The Soul of Man Under Socialism*

A true artist takes no notice whatever of the public. The public to him are non-existent. He leave that to the popular novelist.
> *The Soul of Man Under Socialism*

Purity
What on earth should we men do going about with purity and innocence? A carefully thought-out buttonhole is much more effective.
> *Lady Windermere's Fan*

Questions and Answers
Questions are never indiscreet. Answers sometimes are.
> *An Ideal Husband*

It is always worth while asking a question, though it is not always worth while answering one.
> *An Ideal Husband*

Reformation
The only way a woman can ever reform a man is by boring him so completely that he loses all possible interest in life.
> *The Picture of Dorian Gray*

Relations
I can't help detesting my relations. I suppose it comes from the fact that none of us can stand other people having the same faults as ourselves.
> *The Picture of Dorian Gray*

After a good dinner one can forgive anybody, even one's own relations.
    A Woman of No Importance

Relations are simply a tedious pack of people, who haven't got the remotest knowledge of how to live, nor the smallest instinct about when to die.
    The Importance of Being Earnest

No one cares about distant relations nowadays. They went out of fashion years ago.
    Lord Arthur Savile's Crime

Religion
Religions die when they are proved to be true. Science is the record of dead religions.
    Phrases and Philosophies for the Use of the Young

To die for one's theological beliefs is the worst use a man can make of his life.
    The Portrait of Mr W H

Religion is the fashionable substitute for Belief.
    The Picture of Dorian Gray

Repentance
If a woman really repents, she never wishes to return to the society that has made or seen her ruin.
    Lady Windermere's Fan

Repentance is quite out of date and besides, if a woman really repents, she has to go to a bad dressmaker, otherwise no one believes her.
    Lady Windermere's Fan

Reputation

One can survive everything nowadays, except death, and live down anything except a good reputation.

A Woman of No Importance

One should believe evil of everyone, until, of course, people are found out to be good. But that requires a great deal of investigation nowadays.

A Woman of No Importance

A good reputation is one of the many annoyances to which I have never been subjected.

A Woman of No Importance

Respectability

He must be quite respectable. One has never heard his name before in the whole course of one's life, which speaks volumes for a man, nowadays.

A Woman of No Importance

Romance

Romance is the privilege of the rich, not the profession of the poor.

The Model Millionaire

The worst of having a romance of any kind is that it leaves one so unromantic.

The Picture of Dorian Gray

Nothing spoils a romance so much as a sense of humour in the woman – or the want of it in the man.

A Woman of No Importance

MRS ALLONBY: There is a beautiful moon tonight.
LORD ILLINGWORTH: Let us go and look at it. To look at anything that is inconstant is charming nowadays.
    A Woman of No Importance

Romance should never begin with sentiment. It should begin with science and end with a settlement.
    An Ideal Husband

I am not at all romantic. I am not old enough. I leave romance to my seniors.
    An Ideal Husband

To love oneself is the beginning of a life-long romance.
    Phrases and Philosophies for the Use of the Young

When one is in love one begins by deceiving oneself. And ends by deceiving others. That is what the world calls a romance.
    A Woman of No Importance

Saints and Sinners
The sick do not ask if the hand that smooths their pillow is pure, nor the dying care of the lips that touch their brow have known the kiss of sin.
    A Woman of No Importance

The only difference between the saint and sinner is that every saint has a past, and every sinner has a future.
    A Woman of No Importance

Scandal
I would much sooner talk scandal in a drawing-room than treason in a cellar.
Vera, or The Nihilists

One should never make one's *début* with a scandal. One should reserve that to give an interest to one's old age.
The Picture of Dorian Gray

I love scandals about other people, but scandals about myself don't interest me. They have not got the charm of novelty.
The Picture of Dorian Gray

Gossip is charming! . . . . History is merely gossip. But scandal is gossip made tedious by morality.
Lady Windermere's Fan

LORD GORING: I should fancy Mrs Cheveley is one of those very modern women of our time who find a new scandal as becoming as a new bonnet, and air them both in the Park every afternoon at five-thirty.
An Ideal Husband

School
I have forgotten about my schooldays. I have a vague impression that they were detestable.
An Ideal Husband

Science
Science can never grapple with the irrational. That is why it has no future before it in this world.
An Ideal Husband

Selfishness
Selfishness is not living as one wishes to live, it is asking others to live as one wishes to live.
The Soul of Man Under Socialism

A red rose is not selfish because it wants to be a red rose. It would be horribly selfish if it wanted all the other flowers in the garden to be both red and roses.
The Soul of Man Under Socialism

There are many things that we would throw away, if we were not afraid that others might pick them up.
The Picture of Dorian Gray

The most comfortable chair is the one I use myself when I have visitors.
An Ideal Husband

Self-knowledge
Only the shallow know themselves.
Phrases and Philosophies for the Use of the Young

To know everything about oneself one must know all about others.
The Critic as Artist

Self-sacrifice
Self-sacrifice is a thing that should be put down by law. It is so demoralizing to the people for whom one sacrifices

oneself. They always go to the bad.
An Ideal Husband

Sensitivity
A sensitive person is one who, because he has corns himself, always treads on other people's toes.
The Remarkable Rocket

Serious People
London is too full of fogs – and serious people. Whether the fogs produce the serious people or whether the serious people produce the fogs, I don't know, but the whole thing rather gets on my nerves.
Lady Windermere's Fan

Shakespeare
Shakespeare might have met Rosencrantz and Guildenstern in the white streets of London, or seen the serving-men of rival houses bite their thumbs at each their in the open square; but Hamlet came out of his soul, and Romeo out of his passion.
The Critic as Artist

Sin
Starvation, and not sin, is the parent of modern crime.
The Soul of Man Under Socialism

Sin is a thing that writes itself across a man's face. It cannot be concealed.
The Picture of Dorian Gray

The body sins one and has done with its sin, for action is a mode of purification. Nothing remains then but the recollection of a pleasure, or the luxury of a regret.
The Picture of Dorian Gray

Sincerity

A little sincerity is a dangerous thing, and a great deal of it is absolutely fatal.

> *The Critic as Artist*

Smoking

A cigarette is the perfect type of a perfect pleasure. It is exquisite and it leaves one unsatisfied.

> *The Picture of Dorian Gray*

Gold-tipped cigarettes are awfully expensive. I can only afford them when I am in debt.

> *A Woman of No Importance*

Half the pretty women in London smoke cigarettes. Personally I prefer the other half.

> *An Ideal Husband*

LADY BRACKNELL: Do you smoke?
JACK: Well, yes, I must admit I smoke.
LADY BRACKNELL: I am glad to hear it. A man should always have an occupation of some kind. There are far too many idle men in London as it is.

> *A Woman of No Importance*

Society

What is interesting about people in good society is the mask that each one of them wears, not the reality that lies behind the mask.

> *The Decay of Lying*

Society often forgives the criminal; it never forgives the dreamer.
The Critic as Artist

Society, civilized society at least, is never very ready to believe anything to the detriment of those who are both rich and fascinating.
The Picture of Dorian Gray

LORD CAVERSHAM: Can't make out how you stand London Society. The thing has gone to the dogs, a lot of damned nobodies talking about nothing.
    An Ideal Husband

I love London Society! I think it has immensely improved. It is entirely composed now of beautiful idiots and brilliant lunatics! Just what Society should be.
An Ideal Husband

Other people are quite dreadful. The only possible society is oneself.
An Ideal Husband

Three addresses always inspire confidence, even in tradesmen.
The Importance of Being Earnest.

The Soul
There is no thing more precious than a human soul, nor any earthly thing that can be weighted with it.
The Model Millionaire

Stupidity
There is no sin except stupidity.
The Critic as Artist

Nobody ever commits a crime without doing something stupid.
The Picture of Dorian Gray

Style
In matters of grave importance, style, not sincerity, is the vital thing.
The Importance of Being Earnest.

Suffering
I can sympathize with everything, except suffering. I cannot sympathize with that. It is too ugly, too horrible, too distressing. There is something terribly morbid in the modern sympathy with pain. One should sympathize with the colour, the beauty; the joy of life. The less said about life's sores the better.
The Picture of Dorian Gray

Sunsets
Sunsets are quite old-fashioned. They belong to the time when Turner was the last note in art. To admire them is a distinct sign of provincialism. Upon the other hand they go on. Yesterday evening Mrs Arundel insisted on my going to the window and looking at the glorious sky, as she called it. Of course I had to look at it. She's one of those absurdly pretty Philistines, to whom one can deny nothing. And what was it? It was simply a very second-rate Turner, a Turner of bad period, with all the painter's worst faults exaggerated and over-emphasized.
The Decay of Lying

Superiority
The only thing which sustains one through life is the consciousness of the immense inferiority of everybody else, and this feeling I have always cultivated.
The Remarkable Rocket

Surprise
I am always astonishing myself. It is the only thing that makes life worth living.
A Woman of No Importance

Sympathy
I am always thinking about myself, and I expect everybody else to do the same. That is what is called sympathy.
The Remarkable Rocket

If there was less sympathy in the world there would be less trouble in the world.
The Picture of Dorian Gray

Teachers
Everybody who is incapable of learning has taken to teaching – that is really what our enthusiasm for education has come to.
The Decay of Lying

If you meet at dinner a man who has spent his life in educating himself – a rare type in our time, I admit, but still one occasionally to be met with – you rise from the table richer, and conscious that a high ideal has for a moment touched and sanctified your days. But oh! my dear Ernest, to sit next to a man who has spent his life in trying to educate others! What a dreadful experience that

is! How appalling is that ignorance which is the inevitable result of imparting opinions!
The Critic as Artist

Just as the philanthropist is the nuisance of the ethical sphere, so the nuisance of the intellectual sphere is the man who is so occupied in trying to educate others, that he has never had any time to educate himself.
The Critic as Artist

Tears
The tears that we shed at a play are a type of the exquisite sterile emotions that it is the function of Art to awaken. We weep but we are not wounded. We grieve but our grief is not bitter.
The Critic as Artist

Crying is the refuge of plain women but the ruin of a pretty one.
Lady Windermere's Fan

Temptation
Surely Providence can resist temptation by this time.
Lord Arthur Savile's Crime

I can resist everything except temptation.
Lady Windermere's Fan

Life's aim, if it has one, is simply to be always looking for temptations. There are not nearly enough. I sometimes pass a whole day without coming across a single one. It is quite dreadful. It makes one so nervous about the future.
A Woman of No Importance

There are terrible temptations that it requires strength, strength and courage to yield to.
An Ideal Husband

Thought
Men of thought should have nothing to do with action.
Vera, or The Nihilists

A man who does not think for himself does not think at all. It is grossly selfish to require of one's neighbour that he should think in the same way.
The Soul of Man Under Socialism

All thought is immoral. Its very essence is destruction. If you think of anything, you kill it. Nothing survives being thought of.
A Woman of No Importance

Time
Time is waste of money.
Phrases and Philosophies for the Use of the Young

Town and Country
It is pure unadulterated country life. They get up early because they have so much to do and go to bed early because they have so little to think about.
The Picture of Dorian Gray

Anybody can be good in the country. There are no temptations there. That is the reason why people who live out of town are so absolutely uncivilized. Civilization is not by any means an easy thing to attain to. There are only two ways by which man can reach it. One is by being cultured, the other by being corrupt.

Country people have no opportunity of being either, so they stagnate.
The Picture of Dorian Gray

When one is in town one amuses one's self. When one is in the country one amuses other people.
The Importance of Being Earnest

Personally I cannot understand how anybody manages to exist in the country, if anybody who is anybody does. The country always bores me to death.
The Importance of Being Earnest

Truth
A thing is not necessarily true because a man dies for it.
The Portrait of Mr W H

A truth ceases to be true when more than one person believes in it.
Phrases and Philosophies for the Use of the Young

To know the truth one must imagine myriads of falsehoods. For what is Truth?
The Critic as Artist

If one tells the truth, one is sure, sooner or later, to be found out.
Phrases and Philosophies for the Use of the Young

He would be the best of fellows if he did not always speak the truth.
The Sphinx Without a Secret

It is a terrible thing for a man to find out suddenly that all his life he has been speaking nothing but the truth.
The Importance of Being Earnest

The truth is rarely pure and never simple. Modern life would be very tedious if it were either, and modern literature a complete impossibility.
The Importance of Being Earnest

Tyranny
The history of women is the history of the worst form of tyranny the world has ever known. The tyranny of the weak over the strong. It is the only tyranny that lasts.
A Woman of No Importance

Utopia
A map of the world that does not include Utopia is not worth even glancing at, for it leaves out the one country at which Humanity is always landing. And when Humanity lands there, it looks out and seeing a better country, sets sail.
The Soul of Man Under Socialism

Vanity
Nothing makes one so vain as being told that one is a sinner.
The Picture of Dorian Gray

Vicissitudes
Misfortunes one can endure – they come from outside, they are accidents. But to suffer for one's own faults – ah! – there is the sting of life.
The Critic as Artist

Vulgarity
No crime is vulgar, but all vulgarity is crime. Vulgarity is the conduct of others.
Phrases and Philosophies for the Use of the Young

Vulgarity is simply the conduct of other people and falsehoods the truths of other people.
An Ideal Husband

It is very vulgar to talk about one's business. Only people like stockbrokers do that, and then merely at dinner-parties.
The Importance of Being Earnest

Wagner
I like Wagner's music better than anybody's. It is so loud that one can talk the whole time without people hearing what one says.
The Picture of Dorian Gray

War
As long as war is regarded as wicked, it will always have its fascination. When it is looked upon as vulgar, it will cease to be popular.
The Critic as Artist

Wealth
No man is rich enough to buy back his past.
An Ideal Husband

Every man of ambition has to fight his century with its own weapons. What this century worships is wealth. The God of this century is wealth. To succeed one must have wealth. At all costs one must have wealth.
An Ideal Husband

The Weather
I don't desire to change anything in England except the weather.
The Picture of Dorian Gray

Wickedness
Wickedness is a myth invented by good people to account for the curious attractiveness of others.
Phrases and Philosophies for the Use of the Young

As a wicked man I am a complete failure. Why, there are lots of people who say I have never really done anything wrong in the whole course of my life. Of course, they only say it behind my back.
Lady Windermere's Fan

I hope you have not been leading a double life, pretending to be wicked and being really good all the time, that would be hypocrisy.
The Importance of Being Earnest

Women
Every woman does talk too much.
Vera, or The Nihilists

Women are meant to be loved, not to be understood.
The Sphinx Without a Secret

Never trust a woman who wears mauve, whatever her age may be, or a woman over thirty-five who is fond of pink ribbons. It always means they have a history.
The Picture of Dorian Gray

I am sick of women who love me. Women who hate me
are much more interesting.
The Picture of Dorian Gray

I prefer women with a past. They're always so damned
amusing to talk to.
Lady Windermere's Fan

American girls are as clever at concealing their parents as English women are at concealing their past.
The Picture of Dorian Gray

Women have no appreciation of good looks; at least good women have not.
The Picture of Dorian Gray

I am afraid that women appreciate cruelty, downright cruelty, more than anything else. They have wonderfully primitive instincts. We have emancipated them, but they remain slaves looking for their masters all the same.
The Picture of Dorian Gray

Women, as some witty Frenchman once put it, inspire us with the desire to do masterpieces, and always prevent us from carrying them out.
The Picture of Dorian Gray

It takes a thoroughly good woman to do a thoroughly stupid thing.
Lady Windermere's Fan

It is perfectly brutal the way most women nowadays behave to men who are not their husbands.
Lady Windermere's Fan

I have met hundreds of good women. I never seem to meet any but good women. The world is perfectly packed with good women. To know them is a middle-class education.
Lady Windermere's Fan

Wicked women bother one. Good women bore one. That is the only difference between them.
Lady Windermere's Fan

One should never trust a woman who tells one her real age. A woman who would tell one that, would tell one anything.
A Woman of No Importance

Women – Sphinxes without secrets.
A Woman of No Importance

Good women have such limited views of life, their horizon is so small, their interests are so petty.
A Woman of No Importance

MRS ALLONBY: We women adore failures. They lean on us.
A Woman of No Importance

My dear young lady, there was a great deal of truth, I dare say, in what you said, and you looked very pretty while you said it, which is much more important.
A Woman of No Importance

I don't believe in women thinking too much. Women should think in moderation, as they should do all things in moderation.
A Woman of No Importance

Every woman is a rebel, and usually in wild revolt against herself.
A Woman of No Importance

She looks like a woman with a past. Most pretty women do.
An Ideal Husband

Women have a wonderful instinct about things. They can discover everything except the obvious.
An Ideal Husband

There is only one real tragedy in a woman's life. The fact that her past is always her lover, and her future invariably her husband.
An Ideal Husband

Words
Actions are the first tragedy in life, words are the second. Words are perhaps the worst. Words are merciless.
Lady Windermere's Fan

Work
There is something tragic about the enormous number of young men there are in England at the present moment who start life with perfect profiles, and end by adopting some useful profession.
Phrases and Philosophies for the Use of the Young

The World
The world is a stage, but the play is badly cast.
Lord Arthur Savile's Crime

The world has always laughed at its own tragedies, that being the only way in which it has been able to bear them.
A Woman of No Importance

Worth
Nowadays people know the price of everything and the value of nothing.
The Picture of Dorian Gray

The value of an idea has nothing whatsoever to do with the sincerity of the man who expresses it.
The Picture of Dorian Gray

Youth
Youth is the one thing worth having.
The Picture of Dorian Gray

The secret of remaining young is never to have an emotion that is unbecoming.
The Picture of Dorian Gray

Youth smiles without any reason. It is one of its chiefest charms.
The Picture of Dorian Gray

The youth of the present day are quite monstrous. They have absolutely no respect for dyed hair.
Lady Windermere's Fan

There is nothing like youth. The middle-aged are mortgaged to Life. The old are in life's lumber room. But youth is the Lord of Life. Youth has a kingdom waiting for it. Everyone is born a king, and most people die in exile, like most kings. To win back my youth . . . there is nothing I wouldn't do – except take exercise, get up early, or be a useful member of the community.
A Woman of No Importance